Indianapolis

INDIANA

A PHOTOGRAPHIC PORTRAIT

PHOTOGRAPHY BY

Richard W. Clark

First published in the United States of America by:

Twin Lights Publishers, Inc.
8 Hale Street
Rockport, Massachusetts 01966
Telephone: (978) 546-7398
http://www.twinlightspub.com

ISBN: 1-885435-79-7
ISBN: 978-1-885435-79-8

10 9 8 7 6 5 4 3 2 1

(front cover)
Soldiers' and Sailors' Monument, Monument Circle.

(back cover)
Horse farm in Indianapolis' northwest suburbs.

(frontispiece)
The Pyramids, College Park.

(opposite)
Skyline along Central Canal

Indianapolis' most distinctive feature is the Central
Canal, a scenic water path that flows through down-
town, edged by the beautifully landscaped Canal
Walk. It is the original 19th-century waterway that
connected the city with the outlying village of
Broad Ripple. Along the downtown skyline Chase
Tower and One America Tower stand tall above
the others.

Editorial researched and written by:
Francesca and Duncan Yates
www.freelancewriters.com

Book design by:
SYP Design & Production, Inc.
www.sypdesign.com

Printed in China

Indianapolis was founded along the White River, in 1821, with the hope that it would prosper into a major transportation hub. Unknown to city officials, the river was too sandy for trade. It was not until 1847, when the first railroad to service Indianapolis was completed, that the city began to experience expansive growth. Poised on the original east-west National Road, it quickly developed into a major artery for transportation, connecting Chicago, Cincinnati, and St. Louis.

By the turn of the 20th century, fast-growing Indianapolis was a burgeoning transportation and automobile manufacturing center. In its heyday, the city's Union Station serviced two-hundred trains from eight railroad lines every day, and the area bustled with businesses, hotels, shops, wholesalers, and warehouses.

The antithesis of Detroit's mass-production lines, Indianapolis was the breeding ground of fiercely independent and innovative automobile designers who have created some of the most unique masterpieces of art-deco styling and power in the world, one car at a time. These highly-acclaimed "rolling sculptures" had legendary names such as Dusenberg, Stutz, and Marmon.

Home of the Indy 500

The original racetrack at the Indianapolis Motor Speedway was built as a testing ground for new cars. In 1911, spectators filled the stands for the inaugural Indianapolis 500-Mile Race, the first race of that distance in history. Lap after lap, drivers jockeyed for position at speeds of an unheard-of 75 mph. Driver Ray Harroun in his Marmon "Wasp" battled Lozier driver Ralph Mulford for the grand prize. Harroun won, and the crowds roared. Today, when drivers take off at the annual Indy 500, fans watch the action from around the world.

In addition to auto racing, Indianapolis has earned a national reputation as an auspicious sports center. Home to the 2007 Super Bowl champion Indianapolis Colts, the NBA's Indiana Pacers, the WNBA's Indiana Fever, and the Indiana Ice of the United States Hockey League, the "Hoosier Capitol" supports no less that thirteen major sports facilities.

The Rebirth of Downtown

Like so many American cities in the 1950s, Indianapolis' vibrant downtown core was affected by the dizzying growth of its suburbs. By the 1990s, city planners created a master plan to bring the focus back where it belonged. One of the greatest urban revitalization success stories in the country, Indianapolis' 21st-century refurbishments have brought dazzling cultural, arts, and entertainment districts to areas where only memories of former grandeur existed just a decade before.

Known as the *Crossroads of America*, Indianapolis is alive with sparkling new museums, theaters, art galleries, and new sports arenas. Central Canal's gondolas and singing gondoliers, ethnic restaurants and hot night spots, as well as top-ranked colleges and universities, pristine green-ways, and revitalized downtown residences, mark this thiving metropolis.

With a strong heritage and an eye on the future, Indianapolis is a modern capital city, skillfully molded from a rich historical past. Photographer Richard W. Clark captures this facinating city in detail from glistening night skylines, to period architecture, and vibrant outdoor sculpture. The city of Indianapolis unfolds in this stunning photographic portrait.

Monument Circle (*opposite*)

The Soldiers' and Sailors' Monument is a 284-foot, limestone and bronze monument designed in 1901 by Bruno Schmitz. The statue, located in the center of Monument Circle, honors veterans of the American Revolution, the War of 1812, the Mexican-American War, and the Civil War.

State House Reflections

Reflections of the 1888 State House ripple
on a nearby skyscraper. It is a fitting image
for a building that has seen over one hun-
dred years of Indiana history and controver-
sial legislation that addressed foreign wars,
local politics, and the rights of states,
women, and African Americans.

Golden Eagle

A golden eagle, a symbol of strength and freedom, graces the roof of the Indiana State House. It is one of many magnificent details of this Corinthian-style building. Built in 1888, the interior features an Italian Renaissance décor, that has since undergone major renovations.

Governor Thomas Hendricks (*opposite*)

Rising high on a pedestal amidst a winter wonderland, this statue on the State House grounds commemorates Indiana's sixteenth governor, Thomas Hendricks (1873–1877). Hendricks was also vice president of the United States when Grover Cleveland was in office.

Stained Glass Dome

Rising one-hundred feet above the State House floor, the art glass dome of the Rotunda is the hallmark of this architecturally acclaimed building. With extensive renovations and the addition of artificial light behind the glass, the rich hues of the dome now glow brightly, even on rainy days.

State House Atrium

An extensive restoration has transformed the elegant State House Atrium into a showplace with rich details of the Victorian era. Hallways are lighted with period fixtures and layers of paint were removed from walls and woodworking to expose the beauty of the original surfaces.

Shrine Room *(left)*

A large American flag hangs in the center of the Shrine Room of the Indiana War Memorial Museum. A lighted Star of Destiny shines above the forty-foot marble columns that are set in a circle to represent the defense of America; their deep red color symbolizes blood shed during World War I.

Pro Patria *(right)*

Designed in 1929 by artist Henry Hering, the inspirational *Pro Patria* represents the unflinching spirit of the patriotic soldier. Displayed on the south side of the Indiana War Memorial, the bronze statue depicts a youthful figure, draped in an American flag, reaching heavenward.

Indiana World War Memorial

Covering a full city block, the Indiana World War Memorial pays tribute to veterans who gave their lives during the First World War. It is one of several in downtown Indianapolis' War Memorial Complex that surround Monument Circle.

American Legion Mall *(above)*

Across from the World War Memorial at the
Indiana War Memorial Complex, rows of
flags flutter in the breeze on the American
Legion Mall. Indianapolis is the national
headquarters for the American Legion,
founded here in 1919 by veterans returning
from Europe after World War I.

Veterans Honored *(opposite)*

Massive cylindrical sculptures comprise a
memorial that honors veterans of both the
Vietnam and Korean wars. The Vietnam
portion is slightly larger to illustrate the
greater number of veterans killed or missing
in action. Each soldiers name is engraved
on the memorial.

14

NAM

·973 1964 · 1973 1964 · 1973 1964 · 1973 1964 · 1973

May 20, 1967

Dear Jane,

I'm getting some more prospective about what's going on here. I'm sure that in principle we are doing right, but it's hard to stand by that when a very real DEATH is the consequence in men's struggle for freedom.

Love,
Steve

(Stephen P. Muller)
Killed in Action
July 2, 1967

October 18, 1967

Hi Mom and Dad,

We got some of the best Marines in the world with us here, I wouldn't want to be any place else.

Love always,
Larry

(Ernest L. Bridges)
Killed in Action
April 4, 1968

December 13, 1967

Dear Mom & Dad & all,

Most of us are scared to death, but somebody has to fight this dirty war.

Love always,
Fred (the soldier boy)

(Frederick B. King)
Killed in Action
November 25, 1968

15

Golden Clearing

Storm clouds yield to a hopeful rainbow over downtown Indianapolis. The pot of gold at the end of this rainbow is the dramatically successful revitalization of a vibrant city over the past decade.

Circle Centre Mall (*opposite*)

With an exterior design featuring eight, historic 19th-century building façades, this major shopping, dining, and entertainment complex has the feel of a European street market. Located in the heart of downtown, the Circle Centre Mall is connected to the convention center as well as several hotels.

Old Point Tavern (*above*)

Old Point Tavern, in the heart of Indianapolis' trendy arts and theater district, is a hip and lively pub with music, freshly prepared food, and a cozy atmosphere. During warm weather, the popular outdoor patio makes for great people-watching along Massachusetts Avenue.

Crown Hill Cemetery *(above)*

Crown Hill Cemetery is the highest geographic point in the city. The 1846 burial ground is the third largest in the country. Many notable people are buried here including, James Whitcomb Riley, John Dillinger, and former President Benjamin Harrison.

Southern Circle *(opposite)*

Southern Circle, designed by sculptor Don Gummer, was inspired by Indianapolis' famous Monument Circle. This massive stainless-steel sculpture is located at Meridian Street Plaza, in front of Eli Lilly and Company's Faris Building.

Eli Lilly Global Headquarters

From its modest beginnings in 1876, Eli Lilly and Company has grown into a highly acclaimed, global pharmaceutical giant that employs over 41,000 people worldwide, with over 13,000 in Indianapolis. Over the decades, the Fortune 500 corporation has developed many break-through medicines, including antibiotics and drugs for the treatment of cancer, diabetes, and depression. In 2006, *Fortune Magazine* named Lilly one of the top 100 companies to work for in the United States, and, in 2004, *Working Mothers Magazine* named it a top 10 company for working mothers.

Historic Eli Lilly and Company Building (replica)

Colonel Eli Lilly, a pharmaceutical chemist, came home to Indianapolis after serving in the Civil War and opened his business in 1876 in this modest building on West Pearl Street. Tired of the "magic potions" hawked by sideshow hucksters, Lilly was determined to create high-quality medicines that were real remedies to ailments and, more importantly, were recommended by doctors. With a staff of only three, including his 14-year-old son, he began by improving the quality of existing medicines and later branched out to create new and more effective pharmaceuticals.

Bryan Plays Guitar *(above)*

Bryan Plays Guitar, in White River State
Park, is one of eleven public sculptures by
internationally acclaimed British artist,
Julian Opie. The electrically lit image of
rocker Bryan Adams is over sixteen feet tall.
Opie's mixed-media pieces were displayed
through September of 2007.

Implication of Three - Detail *(opposite)*

This 20-foot-tall ceramic column is located
at the new gateway to Broad Ripple Village,
one of Indianapolis' trendy, cultural districts. Indianapolis artist and teacher Tim
Ryan positioned each of the 650 green and
blue textured tiles to create this inspiring
modern art spectacle.

Indianpolis 500 Festival Parade
(above and left)

One of the best in the country, the parade is the official kick-off of the Indy 500 race weekend. It regularly attracts over 300,000 spectators with its elaborate floats, national celebrities, marching bands, costumed characters, and patriotic units, such as the Medal of Honor veterans above.

St. Patrick's Day Parade *(opposite)*

Formed in 1949, the Indianapolis Murat Highlanders, a marching band of kilt-clad bagpipers and drummers, add their own special music to this much-loved parade as they pass by the imposing Indiana World War Memorial. Festivities begin with the greening of the Central Canal.

Butler University Observatory *(above)*

Butler University, in the historic Butler-Tarkington neighborhood, was named after its 1855 founder, Ovid Butler, an attorney and abolitionist. The Holcomb Observatory and Planetarium is one of the largest public observatories in the world, housing a 38-inch Cassegrain reflector.

University Bell Tower *(opposite)*

Majestic in any season, the Butler University bell tower chimes in Holcomb Gardens, a tranquil area where warmer days find students walking or studying amidst the quiet ponds, canal, and flowering plants and trees.

Obelisk Fountain

Located in the center of the beautifully landscaped Veteran's Memorial Plaza, Obelisk Fountain is dedicated to all Indiana veterans. The one-hundred-foot-tall, Berwick black granite obelisk features four bronze relief panels at its base representing law, science, religion, and education.

Depew Fountain at University Park

The magnificent Depew Fountain in downtown's University Park was designed by sculptor Karl Bitter, who died before it was completed. It was completed by A. Stirling Calder, father of world-famous Alexander Calder. Dancing figures, frogs, and fish adorn all five levels.

University Park

University Park, with the spectacular Depew
Fountain at its center, is a lovely urban park
in the War Memorial Plaza area. The park
features a statue of Indiana native, Presi-
dents Benjamin Harrison and Abraham
Lincoln, and Schuyler Colfax, vice president
under Ulysses S. Grant.

32

University of Indianapolis Esch Hall

Recently expanded Esch Hall is the main admissions office for this private, liberal-arts university. Founded in 1902 by what is now the United Methodist Church, the University of Indianapolis has over 4,000 students, and a curriculum that encourages the application of knowledge to real-world situations.

Herron School of Art and Design

The new Herron School of Art and Design
is a state-of-the-art institution located on
the shared, urban campus of the University
of Indiana and Purdue University (IUPUI).
The new school triples the space of the former quarters, offering a rich curriculum for
students preparing for visual arts careers.

Clowes Memorial Hall

Located on the campus of Butler University, Clowes' stated mission is "lifelong learning in and through the arts." As one of the Midwest's premiere performing arts facilities, Clowes is home to the Indianapolis Opera, Music at Butler, and the Butler Ballet.

Indiana Historical Society *(above)*

Since 1830, the Indiana Historical Society has been the storyteller of the state's extensive and compelling past. This fascinating history center features one of the nation's largest Abraham Lincoln collections. The research library is often used for family genealogy searches.

Union Station *(opposite)*

When it opened in 1853, historic Union Station was the first train station in the world to service more than one railroad line. In its heyday in 1900, it serviced over two-hundred trains a day. Designed in Romanesque Revival style, the station became a national landmark in 1974.

St. John the Evangelist *(opposite)*

The oldest Catholic parish in Indianapolis, St. John the Evangelist Catholic Church was founded in 1837 by Irish immigrants. The building was completed in 1871 and was a former pro-cathedral. Architecturally, the revered landmark is an excellent example of both French-Gothic and Roman styles.

Indianapolis Hebrew Congregation *(above)*

Founded in 1856, the Indianapolis Hebrew Congregation is the oldest Jewish congregation in Indianapolis. Today, Indianapolis is home to more than 40 percent of Indiana's Jewish population.

Summer Celebration

Brilliant fireworks light up the skies over
Indianapolis during the capital city's Fourth
of July celebration, capping off an exciting
day of fun, food, and entertainment along
the Central Canal and throughout the city.
White River State Park celebrates the day
with a food fair, "Taste of Freedom."

Indianapolis Power and Light

The IPL building displays patriotic colors during the city's annual Fourth of July celebration. IPL's predecessors first brought power to Indianapolis in the 1880's. Today, IPL strives to be one of the most environmentally-friendly utilities in the Midwest, serving an area of 528 square miles.

Canal Gondolier *(above)*

Step aboard a gondola and experience a Venice-style boat ride on the Central Canal. In their distinctive black, white, and red costume, gondoliers serenade passengers as they glide along the scenic canal to view the city from a serene and romantic vantage point.

Skyline from Canal Walk *(opposite)*

The magnificent Congressional Medal of Honor Memorial stands along the left bank of the Central Canal. Twenty-seven curved glass walls represent fifteen conflicts, including the Civil War, and display information about the 3,436 Medal of Honor recipients.

Illuminated Turtle (*above*)

A stained glass turtle lights up the night sky in the Broad Ripple neighborhood, one of the city's exciting cultural arts districts. *Turtle* lives next to a bridge on the Broad Ripple Canal. The stylized reptile was designed by local artist David Young of Second Globe Studios.

Indianapolis Artsgarden (*opposite*)

The spectacular seven-story-tall glass Artsgarden hovers over the intersection of Washington and Illinois Streets like a jeweled space craft, providing a spacious performance, exhibit, and marketing space enjoyed by audiences and performers nearly every day of the year.

Indianapolis Artsgarden

Skywalks reaching out in four directions
connect the strikingly beautiful Artsgarden
to adjacent hotels and Circle Centre Mall.
The futuristic glass dome is seven stories tall
and encompasses over 12,000 square feet.
The views of downtown are quite dramatic.

Full Moon Rising

In the 21st century, Indianapolis shines brightly beneath a brilliant full moon. The city has reinvented itself by reinvesting in its downtown area, its heritage and new sports and cultural attractions. As one of America's fasting growing cities, it has a reputation for small-town hospitality.

Circle from Wholesale District

The main street of the historic Wholesale District leads to Monument Circle, where the Soldiers' and Sailors' Monument is decorated for the holidays. Originally a vibrant commercial area surrounding Union Station, the Wholesale District was largely responsible for the growth of the city.

Circle Tower

Circle Tower, a 1930 office building on prestigious Monument Circle, reflects the art deco details that were so popular in the 1920s and 1930s. Historic Landmarks Foundation of Indiana is a dedicated preservation group that helps save and restore old buildings around the state.

Historic Fountain Square

Fountain Square began its first life as an entertainment district with the opening of the Fountain Square Theatre Building in 1928. After decades of steady decline, this historic landmark area has made a comeback as one of Indianapolis' most vibrant arts and entertainment districts.

Bar-B-Q Heaven

This legendary take-out-only barbecue spot is known for its friendly staff and mouth-watering ribs, chicken, shoulder, corned beef, and sweet potato pies. Located a few miles from the Indiana State Fairgrounds, this local favorite continues to maintain a steady flow of patrons.

Strummin' The Blues *(opposite)*

James "Yank" Rachell (1910–1997) had his recording career thrust into motion with his first mandolin at the age of eight. Since then, his music has influenced such giants as B.B. King and John Lee Williamson. Indiana's beloved blues man is honored annually at the Yank Rachell Memorial Blues Festival.

Slippery Noodle Inn *(above)*

The blues are alive and well seven nights a week at the historic Slippery Noodle Inn, Indiana's oldest bar, which opened in 1850. Here, talented local, regional, and national blues bands offer great live performances. The Inn received the Blues Foundation's coveted "Keeping the Blues Alive" award.

Reaching (*opposite*)

Zenos Frudakis' magnificent seven-foot-high bronze figures are reflected in silhouette on the glass façade of downtown office towers. An Indiana native, the acclaimed sculptor has been greatly influenced by classical Greek sculpture and art. His monumental works are in collections around the world.

Citizen 92931 on the Bridge (*above*)

Kevin Huff's striking sculpture on the White River Bridge symbolizes man's never-ending labors. It is one of several works of art, all for sale, in the "Sculpture in the Park" exhibit, sponsored by the White River State Park. The bridge connects the Park with the Indianapolis Zoo.

Indy Jazz Festival *(above)*

The Indy Jazz Festival, produced by the American Pianists Association, was an instant success with big names like B.B. King, Isaac Hayes, and Slide Hampton. Recent festivals have headlined superstars like Bonnie Raitt, Ray Charles, and the Neville Brothers (seen here).

The Vogue *(opposite, top)*

The Vogue, located in Broad Ripple Village, opened in 1938 as a movie theater. Today, it is one of Indianapolis' hottest night spots known for providing not only the best in live entertainment, but for hosting some of the best dance parties in the city.

Hot Summer Juggling *(opposite, bottom)*

The city's premiere arts and theater district, Massachusetts Avenue is a magnet for artists and performers with its prestigeous galleries, public art, and live theater. The tradition began nearly one-hundred years ago when the new Murat Centre introduced live theater to the area.

Twilight Skyline

The sunset washes Indianapolis in a golden glow. The two tallest skyscrapers, Chase Tower on the left and One America Tower on the right, have taken the city skyline to impressive, new heights. The white-capped, brick building in the foreground is part of the Indiana University School of Medicine.

Indiana State Fair

Midway games of chance tempt passersby as the giant ferris wheel takes its riders to the top of the fair. Held every August, the State Fair attracts nearly one million visitors to its rides, live concerts, and agricultural and livestock exhibits. A top feature of the fair is the state Marching Band competition.

Indiana State Museum

The museum began in 1862 with state librarian, R. Deloss Brown and his modest collection of minerals and other curiosities. Since then, the museum has grown beyond natural history, encompassing Indiana art, science, history, and culture, along with traveling exhibits from around the world.

Silent Tribute *(top)*

Snowcapped gravestones pay a silent tribute
to Confederate and Union soldiers. Jefferson
C. Davis is one of thirteen Civil War gener-
als buried in historic Crown Hill Cemetery.
The cemetery is the final resting place for
both the famous and infamous, including
James Whitcomb Riley and John Dillinger.

Historic Waiting Station *(opposite)*

Built in 1885, this structure was originally
the cemetery's administrative offices.
Recently restored by Historic Landmarks of
Indiana, the interior showcases intricately
carved oak and cherry woodwork and other
rich Victorian details, including the first
wooden Venetian blinds in the country.

Civil War Weaponry *(above and opposite)*

At the base of the Soldiers' and Sailors' Monument is the Colonel Eli Lilly Civil War Museum. Archives chronicle the affects of the "War Between the States" on Indiana. One display includes the personal letters and journals of local men and women, as well as public speeches and stories docu-mented from oral histories. Old photographs projected on video screens and exhibits of artifacts, such as muskets and a cannonball fired into a tree, combine to bring a unique understanding of one of America's most difficult periods.

Children's Museum of Indianapolis

Dinosaurs breaking through the Children's Museum of Indianapolis, attract visitors to Dinosphere, the museum's world-class collection of dinosaur fossils. Interactive exhibits on every floor have been engaging young minds since its founding in 1925. Current highlights include SpaceQuest® Planetarium; the world's largest water clock; a prehistoric mastodon found in Indianapolis' backyard; a nine-foot-tall polar bear; an early 20th-century carousel with rare, hand-carved animals; and a prehistoric, ten-ton crocodile.

Eiteljorg Museum *(top)*

The grounds of the Eiteljorg Museum of American Indians and Western Art are enhanced with a stunning, bronze fountain with life-sized, leaping deer. The museum is the only of its kind in the Midwest, and one of two east of the Mississippi that showcases both Native American and Western art.

Indianapolis Art Center *(bottom)*

It began as a WPA project in 1934 with one art teacher and a few students. Today, the institution offers over 250 classes out of a Cultural Complex that also includes artist studios and the Writers' Center of Indiana. Their new ARTSPARK creatively joins art with nature.

Indianapolis Symphony Orchestra

One of the largest performing arts companies in Indiana, the symphony has performed at Carnegie Hall and Washington's Kennedy Center. Over 350,000 people come to its performances every year. Here the Indianapolis Symphony Orchestra skillfully plays during the summer concert series Marsh *Symphony on the Prairie*. The series is sponsored by Marsh Supermarkets and held at the Conner Prairie Amphitheater, in Fishers, Indiana.

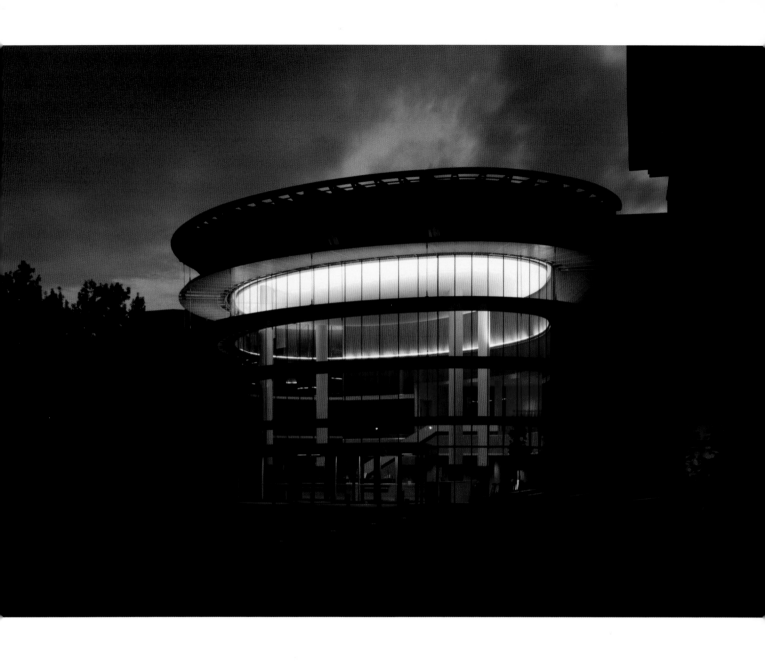

Indianapolis Museum of Art

Founded in 1883, the museum's 50,000-piece collection covers every scope of art history, including ancient Chinese and Japanese art, 18th-century English Masters, French and American impressionism and post-impressionism, modernist Georgia O'Keefe, and cubist Pablo Picasso.

Indiana Roof Ballroom

At its grand opening in 1927, the Roof Ballroom was heralded as the world's most danceable floor. The décor resembled a Spanish coastal village under twinkling stars, clouds, and a crescent moon. After a major renovation, the historic ballroom has been restored to reflect its former grandeur.

Hilbert Circle Theatre

One of America's grand movie palaces of the early 20th century, the Circle Theatre is home to the Indianapolis Symphony Orchestra. With ninety-seven talented members, Indiana's New World Youth Orchestra (*above*) has one of the finest youth symphony programs in the United States.

American Cabaret Theatre *(above)*

When this live musical theater opened in the famous Athenaeum Building on East Michigan Street, it brought the cabaret theatre experience to Indianapolis and, at the same time, saved and restored a century-old, German, architectural masterpiece.

Indiana Repertory Theatre *(opposite)*

Located in a magnificent, landmark building, the Indiana Repertory Theatre has developed into a professional, regional theatre with a varied season of comedy, drama, classics, and contemporary plays. Holiday performances of *A Christmas Carol* are a high point of the season.

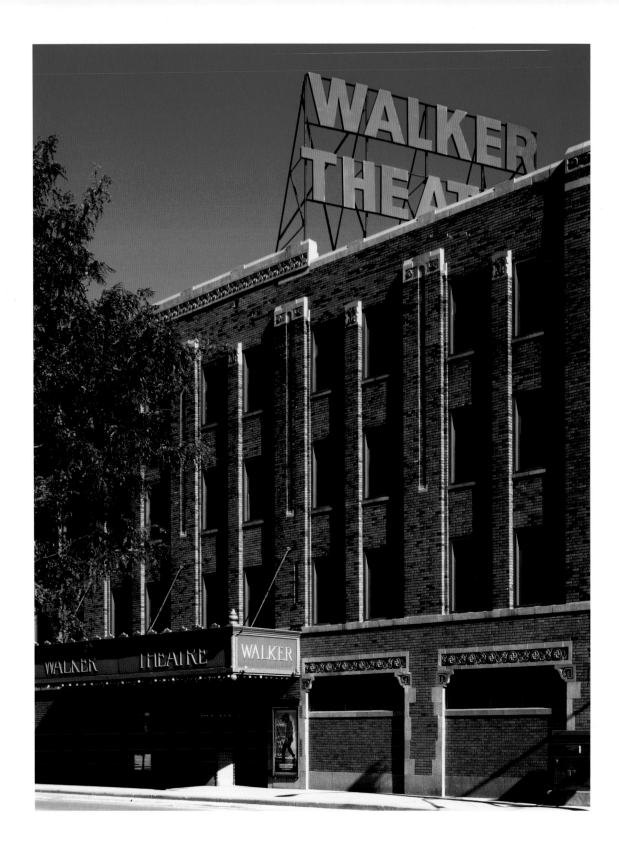

Madame Walker Theatre Center *(above)*

"I am a woman who came from the cotton fields of the South…" This cultural center for African-American arts is named after America's first, female, self-made millionaire and philanthropist. Madame Walker created a manufacturing empire of hair products and cosmetics in the early 20th century.

Jammin' on the Avenue *(opposite)*

African-American sculptor, John Spaulding, celebrates the rich jazz and blues heritage of Indiana Avenue with his fountain sculpture of wind instruments. Saxophones, trumpets, trombones, and sousaphones overlap and intersect as one, creating a fitting vizualizaion of the jazz mystique.

Penrod Arts Fair

Graceful ballerinas entertain the audience
at the annual Penrod Arts Fair, on the
grounds of the Indianapolis Museum of Art.
The fund-raising event benefits local arts
organizations and features music, performing artists, and artworks from more than
300 local and national artists.

Butler Ballet Dancers

Dancers from Butler University's prestigious Butler Ballet company are a living sculpture atop this river rock. The company performs an ambitious season of full-length classical ballets, jazz, and contemporary works in the state-of-the-art Clowes Memorial Hall.

The Ruins at Holliday Park *(opposite)*

Renowned sculptor Karl Bitter, designer of the stunning Depew Fountain in University Park, designed this provocative sculpture for the St. Paul Building in New York City. When the building was later scheduled for demolition, in 1958, arrangements were made to bring the statues to Holliday Park.

Races of Man depict three, life-size statues of kneeling men atop massive columns. On the banks of the White River, the park is environmentally diverse with nearly one-hundred acres of woodlands and trails, native prairie plots, an arboretum, gardens, and the Holliday Park Nature Center.

Murat Centre *(above)*

The Islamic inspired architecture of this former Masonic Shrine boasts a dramatic turret and magnificent tile work. Today, the Murat Centre is an entertainment and events venue that hosts musical groups, Broadway productions, as well as conferences and receptions.

Conner Prairie Living History Museum

Conner Prairie is a living history museum
located in Fishers, Indiana. The museum
depicts different times in Indiana history
with actual artifacts and authentic buildings,
including an 1816 Indian camp, an 1823
homestead, an 1836 pioneer settlement,
and an 1886 Quaker meeting house.

Historic Lilly Mansion

This impressive estate was the home of J.K. Lilly Jr., grandson of the founder of Eli Lilly and Company, the Fortune 500 pharmaceutical giant that is headquartered in Indianapolis. The mansion, located on the grounds of the Indianapolis Museum of Art, displays Lilly's renowned book and coin collections.

Indiana Medical History Museum

The Indiana Medical History Museum features the oldest surviving pathology lab in the country. Located in its original, authentic setting at the former Central State Hospital, the museum includes facinating medical artifacts from the 19th and 20th centuries.

Hook's American Drugstore Museum

Hook's American Drugstore Museum and Soda Fountain features beautiful floor-to-ceiling wood cabinets, countertops, and shelves that are overflowing with original paraphernalia. The mueum reveals 19th-century medical practices as well as the science of soda pop.

President Benjamin Harrison Home (*above*)

Ten rooms in President Harrison's former home now serve as a museum for thousands of presidential artifacts and books. These historical items are displayed among authentic 19th-century furnishings. President Harrison was the twenty-third U.S. president and served from 1889–1893.

James Whitcomb Riley Museum Home (*opposite*)

Noted 19th-century writer and poet, James Whitcomb Riley, was known as the "People's Laureate" and "Children's Poet" with his inspirational poems that touched America. His home, in the historic Lockerbie district, is the only example of late-Victorian preservation open to the public.

Broad Ripple Canal *(pages 86–87)*

This segment of the Central Canal runs through the heart of Broad Ripple Village. The canal, with its extensive greenways and waterways, creates a picturesque country setting for this historic north-side neighborhood.

Victorian Charm *(above)*

The first home of the Indiana Historical Society, this 19th-century Victorian house is in Lockerbie Square, an historic district just seven blocks from the heart of downtown. Lockerbie is a time capsule of Victorian life with block after block of beautifully restored homes dating back to 1847.

Virginia Creeper

A vintage Victorian cottage in the historic Lockerbie neighborhood is overcome with the beautiful wandering vines of Virginia Creeper. It's a fitting metaphor for a community that created an amazing, urban renewal success story.

Eagle Creek Park

There are many ways to enjoy Eagle Creek
Park, one of the country's largest municipal
parks. The spacious lake is perfect for boat-
ing, sailing, and fishing. On shore, visitors
enjoy the "swim beach," biking, hiking, and
the Eagle Creek Nature Center.

Fort Harrison State Park *(top)*

Ice fishing, sledding, and cross-country skiing in winter; walking and jogging down scenic paths in autumn; enjoying woodland wildflowers and bird-watching in spring and summer; or visiting history at the park's two national historic districts are some ways to enjoy this northeast city park all year long.

Fall Creek Canoe Trail *(bottom)*

The tree-lined Fall Creek Canoe trail meananders along for ten miles, from the 79th Street boat launch on Indianapolis' north side. It provides canoeists and kayakers a tranquil and scenic setting to enjoy the outdoors.

Sunset at Eagle Creek Park (*pages 92–93*)

Covering over 4,000 acres, Eagle Creek Park is the city's largest park. It is a favorite with nature enthusiasts who follow the rambling trails through woodlands, brushy areas, grasslands, and along the ponds, creeks, and a reservoir. The park is located just twenty minutes from downtown.

White River Gardens (*above*)

Created in 1988, White River Gardens is a beautiful, botanical attraction adjacent to the Indianapolis Zoo and the White River levee. There are five representative gardens: design gardens, a shade garden, sun garden, water garden, and a wedding garden that provides a perfect setting for outdoor events.

Red Buds and Dogwoods *(top)*

Springtime brings a profusion of blossoming flowers and trees like these dogwoods and redbuds on North Meridian Street, the city's most prestigious address. An historic area, North Meridian has long been the residence of the city's most famous and influential people.

North Meridian Street Home *(bottom)*

North Meridian Street is in an upscale, historic neighborhood in Indianapolis. Spacious, newer homes blend with older ones amidst manicured lawns, creating a much-desired community for the city's well-to-do.

Hilbert Conservatory

The elegant, 65-foot-high glass conservatory houses 5,000 square feet of lush, native plants and trees of the Tropics. Witness a garden just for butterflies, marvel at the ancient craftsmanship of bonsais, or enjoy the Holiday Trainland, one of several seasonal shows.

97

Broad Ripple Fire Station *(above)*

At the heart of Broad Ripple Village is Fire Station No. 32. Built in 1922, the station is a neighborhood landmark. Annexed by the city of Indianapolis, Broad Ripple Village has remained a close-knit community.

Rib America Festival *(opposite)*

Music and barbecue rib lovers unite at the annual Rib America Festival, Indianapolis' Labor Day weekend tradition. Award-winning chefs vie for your taste buds while hot groups like REO Speedwagon, the Charlie Daniels Band, and Hootie and the Blowfish keep you singing and dancing.

Brickhead #3 *(above)*

This provocative and massive sculpture, by Indianapolis native James Tyler, is an audio as well as visual marvel. As viewers approach, a sound track paints an auditory picture of how the brain processes information. Experience it in Davlan Park on Massachusetts Avenue.

City Market *(opposite)*

A small section in Indianapolis was plotted out for market use in 1821. The space continued to develop along with the city as a place to gather and purchase fresh foods. Today, with its new Market District Stage and historic Farmers Market, City Market is a vibrant summer destination.

Monon Trail at White River *(above)*

The busiest part of Indianapolis' fantastic, scenic, greenway system is the Monon Trail. It connects commercial districts, parks, schools, state fairgrounds, and residential neighborhoods. Walkers and joggers take avantage of the Monon Trail regardless of the weather.

Foggy Autumn at Holliday Park *(opposite)*

Leaves of deep, brilliant red stand out among the muted colors in a foggy fall landscape. One of Indianapolis' oldest parks, Holliday Park encompasses over ninety-six woodland acres.

Autumn Chill

The chill of autumn fills the air and a sugar
maple in Fort Harrison State Park trans-
forms from deep greens to brillant reds and
yellows. Before Indiana was settled, dense,
hardwood forests of maple, hickory, oak,
poplar, and sycamore covered eighty-five
percent of the state.

Autumn Leaves

The fall season is heralded in with color and pattern. Leaves of fiery reds, oranges, and yellows pose as nature's fireworks in a fitting farewell to summer. The city of Indianapolis was carved out of prairies and great, dense, deciduous forests.

Early Snow in Eagle Creek Park *(opposite)*

An early October snow adds a frosting to fall leaves before they have had a chance to fall. Indianapolis' winters can be long and cold, with temperatures falling below zero at night and barely rising above freezing during the day. Typical winters deliver two feet of snow.

Suburban Winter *(above)*

A snow-covered horse farm in Indianapolis' northwest suburbs is like a scene from Currier and Ives. The area is experiencing explosive growth and has several of the city's most affluent and desirable neighborhoods along with private and parochial schools of the highest quality.

Northern Cardinal *(opposite)*

Indianapolis' parks are opportune settings
for bird watchers to spot the Northern Cardinal, Indiana's state bird. With binoculars
in hand, birders arrive on foot, as boats are
prohibited in the Marsh and Bird Sanctuary
of Eagle Creek Park.

City Dweller *(above)*

A young, Peregrine Falcon lands upon a
downtown building fire escape. Once an
endangered species, today these birds are
often found in large cities, positioning
themselves on skyscrapers that simulate
cliffs from their natural habitat.

Dolphin Training

Dolphins are a major attraction at the Indianapolis Zoo, the nation's only accredited zoo with an aquarium and botanical garden. The zoo's nine Atlantic bottlenose dolphins live in a spacious, marine environment of over two-million gallons of carefully filtered saltwater and are cared for by a trained staff of marine mammal specialists. The dolphins are the stars of Marsh Dolphin Adventure Theater, where audiences can marvel at these intelligent mammals' natural abilities in a theatrical setting.

Dolphin Adventure Dome

With 360-degree views of the dolphins, this unique dome, resembling a giant air bubble, is the world's first fully-submerged viewing room. Observing from seventeen feet below the surface of the water is a unique perspective, with the dolphins swimming just inches away.

Up Close *(top)*

At the Dolphin Pavilion, you can slip into a wet suit, step into the pool and get up close to these beautiful mammals. This "In-Water Adventure" demonstrates how the trainers teach the dolphins. Interacting with the dolphins is an exhilarating experience.

Indianapolis Zoo *(bottom and opposite)*

Zebras and lions are two of the 360 species waiting to entertain and fascinate at the Indianapolis Zoo, in beautiful downtown White River State Park. The award-winning zoo plays an increasingly important role in worldwide research and conservation. Notably, it was the first zoo in the world to perform successful, artificial insemination of an African elephant. The zoo is separated into five biomes: temperate and tropical forests, water, desert, plains, and encounters, where visitors are encouraged to interact with the animals.

The Indiana Pacers

Fans flock to watch the exciting court action of an Indiana Pacers home game at Conseco Fieldhouse. The NBA team thrills fans season after season with their slam-dunk magic and trips to the NBA playoffs. Women's pro team, Indiana Fever, and the hockey team, Indiana Ice, play here as well.

Conseco Fieldhouse

Built in 1999, Conseco Fieldhouse is the first modern, retro-styled facility in the NBA and has been ranked the top venue in the NBA by *Sports Business Journal*. Between home games, the Fieldhouse hosts concerts, championship wrestling, ice shows, and circus performances.

Little League Promise

A red-capped little leaguer shows great potential on the pitching mound as a future player for the Indianapolis Indians. Indianapolis is a great sports town where enthusiastic fans pack the stands for minor league baseball, professional football, basketball, and hockey.

116

NCAA Hall of Champions

Indianapolis is home to the NCAA national headquarters. The Hall of Champions, part of the NCAA complex, is a spacious facility in downtown White River State Park that celebrates the journey of the NCAA student-athlete.

Victory Field

Indianapolis' new downtown ballpark, Victory Field, has been named "The Best Minor League Ballpark in America" by *Baseball America* and *Sports Illustrated* magazines. It is home to the Indianapolis Indians, the Triple-A affiliate of the Pittsburgh Pirates.

Indiana Colts Football

The beloved Colts have been wowing fans
in the RCA Dome for twenty-two years,
during which time ten Colts players made it
to the Pro Football Hall of Fame. In 2007,
the Colts beat the Chicago Bears in front
of millions of jubilant fans around the world
to become Super Bowl Champions.

2006 AFC Championship Game *(top)*

Indiana Colt fans enter RCA Dome stadium to face the formidable New England Patriots. After trouncing their opponents, the Colts headed to Super Bowl XLI in Miami, Florida and beat the Chicago Bears. It was the team's first Super Bowl Championship in thirty-six years.

Sidewalk Stompers *(bottom)*

The Circle City Sidewalk Stompers Clown Band is a colorful group of twelve accomplished musicians who entertain the crowds at the Indiana Colts AFC championship playoff game. Their 15-minute choreographed show has earned them invitations to play at state fairs across the country.

Number One Fan *(opposite)*

Feeling the spirit of the Colts' AFC Championship win, an enthusiastic fan dances to the beat of the Circle City Sidewalk Stompers Clown Band. The band keeps toes tapping with such favorites as *Zoot Suit Riot* and *It Don't Mean a Thing if It Ain't Got That Swing.*

Indianapolis Motor Speedway Hall of Fame *(above and opposite)*

The thrills are nonstop on and off the track at the famous Indianapolis 500 Speedway. The 96,000-square-foot Hall of Fame Museum is one of the world's most renowned museums dedicated to automobiles and automobile racing. Treasures inside the Hall of Fame include seventy-five legendary cars, many of which have won the esteemed Indy 500, including the Marmon *Wasp*, winner of the first race held in 1911.

National Art Museum of Sport

The National Art Museum of Sport, at University Place, has one of the country's largest collections of sports-related art. Since the private museum moved to Indianapolis, "The Amateur Sports Capital of the World," its note-worthy collection has tripled.

Race Day of the Indianapolis 500

Balloons are released into the air during the opening ceremony of the Indianapolis 500 Mile Race. Prior to the firing of the engines, the song *Back Home Again in Indiana*, is performed by Jim Nabors, thereby signifying the start of the Indy 500.

World Rowing Championships *(top)*

In 1994, the World Rowing Championships came to Indianapolis' Eagle Creek Park. It was the first time this prestigious event was held in an American city. This week-long event attracts the sport's top rowers every year, taking place in different cities around the world.

Mini-Marathon *(bottom)*

The OneAmerica 500 Festival Mini-Marathon is the official start of race season at the Indianapolis Speedway. Live bands, DJs, and dance troupes cheer the 35,000 runners and walkers to the finish line of the country's largest half-marathon.

RCA Championships

Indianapolis is a magical city for sports of all types, including tennis. The prestigious RCA Championships have been named "Tournament of the Year" by the ATP tour players a record eleven times, ten of which were consecutive.

Richard W. Clark

Richard W. Clark is a free-lance photographer based in Indianapolis. He was born and raised in the small town of Carlinville, Illinois, and has been fascinated by nature since childhood. An interest in photography soon followed. After studying zoology at Colorado State University, Richard enrolled in the professional photography program at Colorado Mountain College, and began his career in 1979.

Richard's assignments have taken him all over the world. He has photographed a wide variety of subjects throughout the American West, Alaska, Mexico, Canada, India, Nepal, Pakistan, and Iceland. His images have appeared in many publications including *Audubon, Natural History, The Denver Post, Time,* and *Newsweek.* His photos are also reproduced in calendars featuring Indiana and Indianapolis, and, in 2005, his images celebrating Indiana's natural beauty were published in the large-format book, *Wild and Scenic Indiana.*

Since moving to Indianapolis from Colorado in 1988, Richard has enjoyed shooting a wide variety of corporate, advertising, editorial, and architectural assignments in addition to his nature and travel images. To see more of Richard's work, please visit www.richclarkphoto.com.